AN INTERPRETATION

of

FRANCIS THOMPSON'S

HOUND OF HEAVEN

BY

SISTER MARY DE LOURDES MACKLIN, M.A.

SISTERS OF CHARITY OF NAZARETH

PREFACE BY
BROTHER LEO

NEW YORK, CINCINNATI, CHICAGO, SAN FRANCISCO

BENZIGER BROTHERS

PRINTERS TO THE HOLY APOSTOLIC SEE

TO
THE LITTLE FLOWER OF JESUS
WHO SO LOVINGLY AIDS THE HOUND OF
HEAVEN IN HIS PURSUIT OF SOULS

CONTENTS

PREFACE

THE present work is very appropriately called "An Interpretation" because all vital teaching of literature is interpretative. That does not mean that a great writer is always difficult, cryptic, obscure; it means merely that true literature sounds depths of human experience and human wisdom beyond the reaches of our souls. And this little book is called "*An* Interpretation" because the author, well read in books, experienced in life and alive to school conditions, realizes that there is no one interpretation of any literary masterpiece.

One way of telling a great book from a book of lesser importance is to observe that the great book may be read any number of times with profit and with pleasure, while the little book, when read once, is definitely finished. The little book has substance, but not much; it has style, but that style is limited in scope and in appeal; it has mood, but the mood is one and weak and unvaried. The great book, on the other hand, possesses some of that paradoxical unity of simplicity and complexity so characteristic of human life and so characteristic of the artistic products emanating from human life. Little books are like the pond which every winter forms outside this pleasant window where I am now writing; great books are like the ocean, sometimes calm, sometimes stormy, sometimes blue and sometimes gray; that ocean which is at once a challenge, an adventure, a playmate, a tyrant, an inspiration and an ever-shining goal.

Francis Thompson's "Hound of Heaven" is a great poem, certainly the greatest individual poem that the nineteenth century produced; and because it is great it gives itself to almost infinite interpretation. Not the least mark of its greatness is that it touches upon phases of human life and human experience drawn from every condition of society and from every stage of moral and religious development. One might even say that here the poem is greater than the poet. It is a mystic mirror into which the old man, the man of affairs, the housewife, the nun, the saint, and the unassuming child may all gaze and find a reflection of their essential selves. It is not merely a spiritual portrait of Francis Thompson; it is a spiritual portrait of humanity and of all individual men.

Sister Mary de Lourdes' study will bring students to realize that literature in general and poetry in particular demands personal interpretation. It will bring them close to the heart of books; and the heart of books is the heart of humanity. And the heart of humanity—what is that but the glowing truth that man was created for God and knows no surcease until in God he rests?

BROTHER LEO

SAINT MARY'S COLLEGE,
CALIFORNIA.

INTRODUCTION

WITH a feeling of awe and reverence, as if tread-
ing on holy ground, one approaches the study
of "The Hound of Heaven," the greatest poem in the
English tongue and the greatest ode of all time: great,
not because of its perfect diction, exquisite imagery
and soul-stirring passages, but because of its theme,
the highest, holiest theme that the human mind can
conceive—the love of God for man, the love of the
Almighty, Eternal, All-Holy God for poor, weak, sin-
ful man.

Who can measure the height, the depth, the immen-
sity of that love, a love which existed before the
heavens and the earth, and will exist unchanged for all
Eternity; "I have loved thee with an everlasting love,"[1]
a love that has manifested itself in our creation, re-
demption, preservation, in a thousand different ways?

A poem with such a theme can never die. This
sublime song, the most sublime that ever fell from
uninspired lips, will live as long as there are human
souls to suffer and human hearts to love—aye, its

> "Echoes roll from soul to soul
> And grow forever and forever."[2]

The life story of a soul in its search for happiness
is of universal appeal. "The Hound of Heaven" por-

[1] Jer. xxxi. 3.
[2] Tennyson, Bugle Song.

trays a soul that has faith in God and knows His love, yet flees that good God and His infinite love. And why? Because the poor deluded one's heart is set on creatures and he cannot endure the thought of giving them up. He has heard that God is "a jealous God"[3] and that "No man can serve two masters."[4]

Eagerly we follow the erring one in his wanderings, lured hither and thither by false lights, as a belated traveler is led astray by the treacherous will o' the wisp. Pityingly we see him fleeing from Truth, Beauty and Goodness, and embracing their counterfeits; but while commiserating the blindness or condemning the folly of the misguided one, the humiliating realization dawns upon us that we are gazing upon a more or less perfect image of ourselves and our weaknesses and infidelities. But for Our Heavenly Father's preventing grace, should we not all follow wandering fires and fall into snares and pitfalls that beset our way through this valley of tears?

What is the soul seeking? Happiness. In every human heart there is a desire for happiness, a craving which is a part of man's nature, hence from God. This desire can be gratified, else God would not have implanted it in the heart of man. The quest for happiness continues from the cradle to the grave. But alas! many seek for it where it cannot be found; in wealth, in pleasure, in honor, in human affection. Riches may take wings and fly away, or prove a splendid misery; pleasures, like Dead Sea apples, turn to ashes at the touch; friends may prove untrue or leave us desolate;

[3] Deut. v. 9.
[4] Matt. vi. 24.

fame like an iridescent bubble, vanish at a breath. None of these are satisfying, even at their best. The heart can find rest in God alone. It was made for Him and small though it be, all things else cannot fill it. One who seeks perfect content away from its true source, is consciously or unconsciously fleeing from God.

I

THE FLIGHT

THE inadequacy of creatures is well portrayed in "The Hound of Heaven." In the first stanza we have, as it were, a summary of the whole story: the soul enticed by false promises, climbs the deceptive heights of earthly glory, worldly joy, only to be hurled into an abyss of disappointment and gloom. It is there that the divine Comforter comes to its aid.

The keynote of the tragedy is struck in the first three words, "I fled Him." This is the candid, humble acknowledgment of a disenchanted soul, a triple wail of sorrow and repentance, a repentance that seems to grow deeper at each repetition of the confession.

"I fled Him down the nights and down the days." As all directions from the North Pole are south, so all directions from God are down. By Baptism, the soul is placed on the radiant heights with God, and there, bright and beautiful from the regenerating waters,

> "In that sweet age
> When Heaven's our side the lark,"[1]

it basks in the light of its Father's smile and is held by its Father's hand. The innocent child, all unconsciously, is ever giving glory to its Maker. Only when reason

[1] Francis Thompson, In Darkest England.

holds sway, however, will it be capable of conscious praise, of offering immediate homage to its Creator, of thanking Him, loving, adoring, serving Him. Oh! but will it pay homage to its sovereign Lord? Who can answer?

Man, the only being endowed with intellect and free will, hence the only creature that is capable of glorifying God, is the *only one* that fails to give Him glory, the only one that refuses to do His will. Often he turns his God-given powers against the giver, or shuns Him as an enemy and seeks refuge and solace in creatures. Having torn himself away from the restraining hand of a loving Father, he goes down from the sunny, peaceful heights, wanders into a foreign land and wastes his substance.

> "I fled Him down the nights and down the days,
>   I fled Him down the arches of the years."

That is, at all times, in darkness and light, joy and sorrow. There is no halting, no looking back, no regrets. He, Mansoul, as we shall call him, keeps his eyes fixed on the future. He sees the years stretching out before him like the arched naves of vast cathedrals, perfect in their symmetry, graceful in outline, each more beautiful than the last; and eagerly he hastens on and on.

> "I fled Him down the labyrinthine ways of my
>   own mind."

The mind of man, the wonderful power of reasoning, places him as far above irrational creatures as the heavens are above the earth, aye, next to the angels.

"What a piece of work is man!
How noble in reason, how infinite in faculty!
. . . In apprehension how like a god!"[2]

Man is distinctively man by his intellect and will. By our intellect we can know God, and by our will, guided by our intellect, we can love Him. If we love Him we shall serve Him and so attain the end of our creation, perfect happiness. By using these great faculties rightly, we give glory to God, and direct the material creation to His service. Mansoul would use his marvelous powers for an unworthy end. Knowing the influence of the intellect on the will, he tries by false and subtle reasonings, to cause the will to deviate from its duty. By specious arguments he would prove that there is no such thing as accountability, that man is a free agent and can do as he pleases. He blinds himself to the fact that man, though physically free, is not morally so.

He becomes hopelessly entangled in a labyrinth of false philosophy, and, guided by its pernicious principles, would persuade himself that he can hide from God, even "in the midst of tears," forgetting that sorrow and suffering form a straight road to Him. He might expect to hide "under running laughter," for amid the joys of life, one does not feel so much the need of divine help. Creatures seem to suffice. Yet in tears and smiles, sorrow and joy, we need the all-tender, sympathetic Friend who soothes our sorrows and intensifies our joys.

"Up vistaed hopes I sped."

[2] Shakespeare, Hamlet.

Roseate-hued hope opens to the wondering eyes of youth, bright vistas, vistas to a future of cloudless skies and deathless flowers, with a shining pathway leading to the heart's desire. Does the youth wish for pleasure? Pleasure, the siren, is there beckoning him on to her delightful groves and flowery fields. Does he wish for riches? The hills are purest emeralds, and the rivers, molten gold. Does he crave fame? There on the rainbow-crowned heights is the airy temple in which his name shall be emblazoned on high.

Hope is a strong beautiful barque which speeds lightly before the wind, weathers the fiercest gale, and rides safely through the rocks and shoals when the anchor is to be cast only in the bright harbor of Eternity. But when one has the perishable things of earth for the goal of his hopes, he finds himself

". . . precipitated
Adown Titanic glooms of chasmèd fears."

The courage, born of hope, dies, giving place to despondency, even despair, whose darkness enshrouds the soul and hides the star of hope entirely from view.

Mansoul tries to persuade himself that in the depths of the chasm he will escape "from those strong Feet that followed, followed after," but to his great dismay, it is here that the dauntless Lover overtakes him. It is when he lies at the bottom of the abyss, bruised and bleeding, shorn of all that the world holds dear, that he is found by his Pursuer. Broken and helpless, he is at His mercy and must needs listen to the unwelcome words: "All things betray thee, who betrayest Me." How canst thou expect My creatures to be faithful to thee when thou art unfaithful to their Creator? The works of My hand are true to Me when they do My will. It is My will that they satisfy not the cravings of the heart, so that My children whose love I long for, will have to turn to Me. Were thy will conformed to Mine, all things would be conformed to thine, hence would not betray thee.

Blessed indeed is the soul that in the dark hour of trial, hearkens to the voice of God whether chiding or consoling, and abandoning herself to Him, throws herself into His arms. Sorrow and suffering have brought many a wanderer back to his Father's house.

> The "unhurrying chase,
> The unperturbèd pace,
> Deliberate speed, majestic instancy,"

show forth the omnipresence of God, "in whom we live and move and have our being."[3] No effort is needed to overtake the fleeting soul, for He is always with it, waiting calmly, patiently, for the first sign of repentance, that He may clasp it to His bosom.

The father of the Prodigal, though he mourned the departure of his erring son and welcomed him with joy on his return, did not go with him into that far country, and remain with him, to aid and comfort, cheer and bless, as our loving Father remains with His children. Such devotion in an earthly father is hardly conceivable. Though the good shepherd went in search of his lost sheep and brought it back rejoicing, he did not follow it when it strayed away, as the Divine Shepherd follows the lambs of His flock. No earthly love can fully symbolize the all-embracing love of God.

[3] Acts xvii. 28.

II

ILLUSIONS AND DISILLUSIONS

THE passions are like spirited horses which if well controlled will carry the traveler swiftly and safely to his destination; but left unchecked, will lead him to destruction. Love, the strongest of all the passions, is the greatest motive power in the world. It is love, but, sad to say, inordinate love that sways the soul in "The Hound of Heaven." He knows no hate, loves nothing sordid or low. He has lofty ideals and noble aspirations, though in his blindness he misses the highest and best. We cannot help pitying him in his disillusions, loving him in spite of his faults, as we would an irresponsible child, and rejoicing with him in his conversion—we might say resurrection from the grave of self-love. How the all-loving Father must cherish such a guileless spirit, even when it is apparently fleeing from Him.

Mansoul loves his fellow men and longs for love in return, so he knocks for admission at the doors of their hearts, kind, loving hearts,

> "A hearted casement curtained red,
>   Trellised with intertwining charities."

He pleads "outlaw-wise," as one cut off from human sympathy; yes, begs for human affection though he knows the "love of Him who follows." Why does he

avoid such a Lover? The answer to this question is the
reason for the flight,

> "I was sore adread
> Lest, having Him, I should have naught beside."

The same dread deters many souls from climbing the
heights of sanctity, even from starting on the road to
perfection. If they would but reflect on the reassuring
words of Our Lord, "Seek ye first the Kingdom of God
and His Justice and all things else will be added unto
you,"[1] how different would be their lot? The more we
love God the more perfectly we love those dear to us,
as we love them in God and for God. "Little casement"
is very expressive, emphasizing the contrast between
human and divine love—the one so narrow, so little;
the other an ocean that hath no limit. Mansoul, dis-
appointed in his high hopes of obtaining that which he
had conceived to be the solace of all his sorrows, the
doubling of all his joys, turns away, sad and dispirited,
from the closed casement. Happy for him were he wise
enough to profit by the lesson taught by his disappointments and seek admission into that Heart which would
never close against him; where he would find the fulfil-
ment of all his desires, the realization of all his hopes.
But alas! that tender, loving Heart is the very one he is
fleeing from. In his eager search for happiness, he is
going far from its true source. Whither shall he turn?
The unloving world has rejected him, so he lifts his
eyes to the heavens. Oh! if the eyes of his soul would
but see the Heaven of heavens! As he gazes upward

[1] Matt. vi. 33.

he is enthralled by the glory of the midnight sky; the soft beauty of the moon and the splendor of the thousands of stars charm his heart, hold him entranced. As the brilliant orbs smile tenderly upon him, a great love of beauty takes possession of him and he exclaims in rapture, "Ah! I have found the true source of joy. In thee, O Beauty, shall I seek my rest." "Love has but one cause and that cause is beauty."[2]

So with hopes revived, this eager soul flies "across the margent of the world." "Plays truant from earth, slips through the wicket of fancy into heaven's meadows."[3] He troubles

> "The gold gateways of the stars,
>   Smiting for shelter on their clangèd bars."

Humbly had he pleaded for admission into the hearts of men, he *demands* admittance into the heart of beauty, yes, not only demands it but endeavors to obtain it by force, "The soul striking the sublime stars, the intolerable passion for beauty."[4] He frets

> "To dulcet jars
> And silvern chatter the pale ports of the moon."

Again he is outlawed. The starry spheres, faithful to the Maker,

> "Forever singing as they shine
>   'The hand that made us is divine,' "[5]

[2] Lacordaire.
[3] Francis Thompson, Shelley.
[4] Mr. Garvin, Francis Thompson in *Bookman*, March, 1897.
[5] Addison.

have nothing in common with him. He turns a deaf ear
to their praises of the divine Artist. He will not listen to

> "The burning rhetoric and quenchless oratory
>   Of the magniloquent and all-suasive sky."[6]

He grows weary of the stars, and longs for the day-
spring to quench their fires, so he calls on dawn, "Be
sudden." He hopes that bright, smiling Aurora will
welcome him with open arms, robe him in saffron and
gold, crown him with diamonds and give him to banquet
with her

> "In her wind-walled palace
>   Underneath her azured dais."

But she also is a faithful subject of the King, and
pleases only those who serve her Master.

The fleeting splendors of dawn soon give place to
the glorious sun, that wondrous source of light and
beauty, and Mansoul exclaims:

> "High in thine ancient pomp inaugural
>   Wide o'er rout-trampled night,
>   Flew-spurned the pebbled stars."

> "Thou swayest thy sceptered beam
>   O'er all delight and dream,
> Beauty is beautiful but in thy glance."[7]

But the searching light of the garish sun becomes
more unendurable than

> "The abashless inquisition of each star"[8]

[6] Francis Thompson, To Stars.
[7] Francis Thompson, The Setting Sun.
[8] Francis Thompson, Sister Songs, Part I.

and in order to hide from it he begs of eve

> "Be soon.
> With thy young skyey blossoms heap me over
> From this tremendous Lover."

More and more he realizes the love of Him that follows, and more and more he tries to evade Him. He
fain would hide himself among the stars, but remembers
that they are God's forget-me-nots;

> "The heavens declare the glory of God
> And the firmament showeth forth His handiwork."[9]

He hopes to escape in the darkness of the night, the
keen eyes of his Pursuer.

> "Float thy vague veil about me lest He see."

"Perhaps darkness shall cover me."

"But darkness shall not be dark to Thee, and night
shall be light as the day: the darkness thereof and the
light thereof, are alike to Thee."[10] Sun, moon, stars,
darkness, all irrational creatures are true to their Maker
and will not conspire against Him. They do not try to
serve two masters.

> "In faith to Him their fickleness to me,
> Their traitorous trueness and their loyal deceit."

Poor Mansoul finds that "The rays of the stars are
like thorns to flowers, and the poet after wandering
over heaven, returns with bleeding feet."[11] He exclaims: In thee, O Beauty, I thought to find rest to my

[9] Ps. xviii. 2.
[10] Ps. cxxxviii. 11, 12.
[11] Francis Thompson, Shelley.

soul, but thou hast sworn allegiance not to me but to Him from whom I flee.

Poetry will surely not disappoint me, for

"Poetry is in itself strength and joy."[12]

There shall I find my delights.

On the bright pinions of fancy he flies far beyond the boundaries of sense into the empyrean blue and with Shelley

"Runs wild over the fields of ether"[13]

borne hither and thither as imagination wills,

"Clings to the whistling mane of every wind."

But whether carried by the winged steed of inspiration through the calmer regions of poetry, "The long savannahs of the blue," or by an ambitious Pegasus aloft to the awful heights of grandeur and sublimity, where

"Thunder-driven
They clang his chariot athwart a heaven
Plashy with lightnings around the spurn of
    their feet."

He cannot elude the insistent Lover. God is there. Poetry is the expression of beauty and God is the "Beauty ever ancient and ever new."[14] "Poetry is in itself a thing of God. He made His prophets poets, and the more we feel of poesy do we become

'Like God in love and power.' "[15]

Mansoul flees frantically from his persevering Pursuer and to hasten his flight "Clings to the whistling

[12] *Ibid.*   [13] *Ibid.*   [14] St. Augustine.   [15] Bailey.

mane of every wind." Yet the following Feet ever keep pace with him.

"If I climb up into heaven Thou art there, if I go down into hell Thou art there also. If I take the wings of the morning and remain in the uttermost parts of the sea, even there also shall Thy hand lead me and Thy right hand shall hold me."[16] Above the sound of footsteps is heard the warning Voice, "Naught shelters thee who wilt not shelter Me." Human hearts have refused him admission. Beauty and Poetry are too true to their divine origin to shelter those at enmity with their Author.

Heeding not the warning Voice, Mansoul continues in his mad career. Happiness must be found. The desire for it has become an all-absorbing passion. He must find

> "Happiness, our being's end and aim—
> Good, pleasure, ease, content—whate'er thy
> name."[17]

Where now shall he seek for it? The smile of innocent childhood solves the problem.

> "But still within the little children's eyes,
> Seems something, something that replies.
> *They* at least are for me, surely for me."

How pathetic is the forlorn hope expressed in this cry from a heart that is growing accustomed to disappointments! He turns, very wistfully, to the children. Longingly, imploringly, he begs their love and confidence. Shall he not silence that imperative Voice, those

[16] Ps. cxxxviii. 8-10.   [17] Pope, Essay on Man.

awful footsteps, in their childish prattle and loving caresses? In their young eyes, he sees dawning answers, answers to all his longings, all his questionings, all his hopes. Fair indeed do their eyes seem to him when he reads such messages in their liquid depths, and he rejoices in the thought that he has found the object of his search. But ere those messages are expressed, "Their angel plucks them by the hair." Childhood is as fleeting as the spring-time.[18] Scarcely do the snowdrop and violet announce the coming of spring, ere she melts into summer. So with evanescent childhood. Just when we are most charmed with "the sweet feat ways" of a child, relentless time robs us of our treasure, giving us in its place a man or woman with the cares and responsibilities of manhood or womanhood. The full-blown rose may be more beautiful than the bud but it is not the bud and never will be.

[18] That this is Francis Thompson's meaning of "Their angel plucks them by the hair," may be inferred from the following: "Our very gentleness to our children is because we know how short their time. 'Eat,' we say, 'eat, drink and be merry; for to-morrow ye are men.'" *Moestitiae Encomium.*

> "Now at one and now at two,
> Swift to pout and swift to woo,
> The maid I knew.
> Still I see the duskèd tresses
> But the old angers, old caresses?
> Still your eyes are autumn thunders,
> But where are you, child, you?"
> *To Monica after Nine Years.*

III

THE LAST RESORT

THE poor soul, wearied of its vain efforts to find happiness in friendship, beauty, poetry, all that appealed most to him, even in children that he thought were surely for him, turns pleadingly to Nature's children. These at least are his for the asking. No one can deprive him of them, for Nature never grows old. Renewing her youth like the eagle, she is ever young, ever fresh, ever fair. Her "azured dais" is as bright and beautiful as when first "The morning stars sang together";[1] the sun is as active, the clouds as varied, the flowers as fragrant, all Nature as beautiful as when she came from the hand of God.

Yea, this glorious earth is all his own, with its smiling valleys, flower-strewn fields, snowy peaks, laughing cascades and oceans sublime. Surely here is everything to satisfy the most fastidious. Nature will not close her great warm heart against him. She will sympathize with him in all his moods and bring sweet solace to his soul, for

> "To him who in the love of nature, holds
>   Communion with her visible forms, she speaks
> A various language; for his gayer hours
>   She has a voice of gladness and a smile

[1] Job. xxxviii. 7.

> And eloquence of beauty; and she glides
> Into his darker musings with a mild
> And healing sympathy, that steals away
> Their sharpness ere he is aware."[2]

Despite his apparent enthusiasm, however, one who runs may read that Mansoul turns to Nature as a last resort.

> "Come *then* ye other children, Nature's—share
> With me (said I) your delicate fellowship."

"My last and only hope of happiness is in you." How earnestly he pleads,

> "Let me greet you lip to lip
> Let me twine with you caresses."

Heart and soul he enters into this new alliance giving himself unreservedly, offering undivided homage to Mother Nature, acknowledging her as all-sufficient, a sovereign whose laws account for the manifold wonders of the Universe. He sports joyously with her children, making himself one of them. "He stands in the lap of patient Nature and twines her loosened tresses after a hundred wilful fashions."[3] He feasts on the beauties which he finds everywhere "in her wind-walled palaces."

> "With beauty's importunacy
> All things plead 'We are fair.' "[4]

[2] Bryant, Thanatopsis.
[3] Francis Thompson, Shelley.
[4] Francis Thompson, Carmen Genesis.

He takes delight in penetrating her secrets and finds it not only a delightful but an easy task.

> "I start
> Thy secrets lay so bare."[5]

> "*I* knew all the swift importings
> On the wilful face of skies."

This wilful face of the sky with its ever-changing expression, charms him. He loves the cloudless blue, so calm, so serene, so soothing, and he loves still more that blue diversified with clouds; soft, feathery cirrus, the gorgeous sunset clouds, the great snowy masses, and the fierce storm-cloud, black, ominous, flashing with defiance and muttering in its wrath.

He is delighted when the sun, repenting of having burnt the fair cheek of Nature with his ardent kisses, draws water from the streams and the seas,

> "Spumed of the wild sea-snortings"

and bids the winged winds bear it o'er the land,

> "To bring fresh showers for the thirsting flowers."[6]

He rejoices in Nature's joy, and sorrows in her sorrow.

> "All that's born or dies
> Rose and drooped with."

His mood varies with her mood. He is glad at the birth of a flower, a day, a year, and mourns their death.

> "I was heavy with the even,
> When she lit her glimmering tapers
> Round the day's dead sanctities";

[5] Francis Thompson, Ibid.   [6] Shelley, The Cloud.

round its departed glories, the roseate hues of sunset, the gleam of lake and stream, the exquisite coloring of forest and field, and the sweet smiles that lighted the faces of the flowers as they looked into their mother's eyes. All have perished with the day.

He is ecstatic with joy when the new day is enthroned and with the awakening earth, he exclaims, *"Le roi est mort, vive le roi."* He mingles his smiles with the sunshine and his tears with the raindrops.

"Heaven's sweet tears were salt with mortal mine."

"Against the red throb of its sunset heart
        I laid my own to beat,
        And share commingling heat.
But not by that, by that, was healed my
        human smart."

He has been giving all: love, sympathy, tenderness, and he looks for the same in return; but alas! he receives nothing but coldness, indifference, harshness. The depth of the suffering, the anguish, caused by his repeated disappointments is manifest for the first time in the words, "human smart." He hoped to find in Nature the panacea of all his woes, but that hope, like all the rest, has perished. His tears and sighs make no impression on her. She knows not, cares not what he says. They understand not each other. He speaks in sounds, she in silences.

"You speak and you think she answers you, it is the echo of your own voice. You think you hear the throbbing of her heart and it is the throbbing of your own. I do not believe that Nature has a heart."[7]

[7] Francis Thompson, Nature's Immortality.

He expected to find in her a kind mother and realizes that she is an unfeeling step-mother who refuses a refreshing draught to a poor soul perishing of thirst, a burning thirst which for years he has tried to quench.

> "Never did any milk of hers once bless
> My thirsting mouth."

Why did this poor lonely soul find no rest, no sympathy, no happiness in Nature, when others do? Because "She is God's daughter and stretches forth her hand only to her Father's friends."[8]

Nature has failed him because he is faithless to God. She would have led him, had he been docile to her inspirations, to the fountain of living waters where he could have slaked his burning thirst. Her eloquent silence would have spoken to him of her Father and his Father; of the wisdom, power, beauty, goodness of

> "The Eternal One whose presence bright
> All space doth occupy, all motion guide."[9]

But he turns a deaf ear to her entreaties. He wants *her* sympathy, not that of her Maker. Unconsciously to himself, however, she has brought him to the feet of God as she has brought many a wanderer. "Nigh and nigh draws the chase." The long flight is over. Desolate, disillusioned, the poor fugitive, driven to the wall, stands like a stag at bay. His Pursuer is upon him. He must listen now, however reluctantly, to the Voice he has fled for years;

" 'Lo, naught contents thee who content'st not Me.' "

[8] Francis Thompson, Ibid.   [9] Derzhavin, God.

The cause of the failure of his quest is beginning to dawn upon him. He has been chasing phantoms instead of realities, shadows for the substance, so has never found content, the happiness he sought. Creatures have their limitations set by their Creator, and they are faithful to their limitations. They are finite and cannot fill the heart of man, small though it seem, because it is made for the infinite and nothing less than the infinite can satisfy it.

IV

Conditional Surrender

CREATURES content man only so far as he contents God, that is, when seeing God in the works of His hands, he uses them as stepping-stones to his last end. Mansoul, dazzled by reflections, has been fleeing the source of light, "That was the true Light that enlighteneth every man that cometh into the world."[1] Now for the first time he faces the Light and sees his own nakedness.

"Naked, I wait Thy love's uplifted stroke."

Stripped of all earthly hopes, thwarted in all his desires and affections, humbled by the consciousness of his helplessness, his nothingness, smitten to the knee, he is ready to surrender to the love he has shunned so long.

Hitherto he has looked only to the future, lured on and deceived again and again by the mirages that appear in the desert of life, never turning to look at the road he had been traveling. Now he gazes upon the past and sees the ruin of the years,

"In the rash lustihood of my young powers,
I shook the pillaring hours
And pulled my life upon me; grimed with smears
I stand amid the dust o' the mounded years—
My mangled youth lies dead beneath the heap."

[1] John. i. 9.

Strong in the strength of his youth, he, like another Samson, had pulled away the pillars that supported the beautiful arches of the years and his youth lies dead beneath the wreckage. Sadly now he looks upon a wasted life. He bewails lost opportunities. He sees again his boyhood days and the two roads that lay before him, "the primrose path of dalliance"[2] and the hard way of the cross: this, steep, narrow and rocky, beset with thorns and briers; that, broad, and smooth and pleasant; in this, the blood-stained footprints of the thorn-crowned Man of Sorrows; in that, the bright roses of love and joy; in this, sad misereres and tears of compunction; in that, merry laughter and song. The one, he knew, led to Heaven and God Himself was the pilgrim's guide. The other led he knew not where, but the attractions it presented were so varied that it seemed to him a paradise. Little he knew that "The trail of the Serpent was over them all."[3] He feared that in the thorny way he would have naught but God; and God's creatures were so delightful, so charming to him. He would choose the noble, the good, the most like God— but alas! *not* God. And now?

> ". . . Grimed with smears
> I stand amid the dust o' the mounded years."

Surely with such proofs of his folly and infidelity staring him in the face, he is humbled to the dust. His renunciation must be complete. No, there is rapine in the holocaust. As a dying man grasps at a straw, he would grasp the dream that is flying from him, and he

---

[2] Shakespeare, Hamlet.
[3] Thomas Moore, Paradise and the Peri.

would draw music from the lute that has been such a comfort to him. All in vain! "Even the linked fantasies" are deserting him. He had hoped that when all else would leave him, he would have at least intellectual pleasures; be able to revel in the fields of the mind; to gather flowers there that would delight him with their beauty and fragrance. The earth was the plaything of his imagination. Entangled in the meshes of his fertile fancy, it had swung a trinket at his wrist. "His playthings are those that the gods give their children. The universe is his box of toys."[4]

But the world has grown heavy with sadness, too heavy for the weak words of his fancy. The ethereal spirit, Poesie, has deserted him. He had looked to her for consolation in his loneliness. She could have given him a world of his own to live in, a beautiful world of visions, when the real world has abandoned him.

This supreme sacrifice brings forth the wail:

> "Ah, is Thy love indeed
>   A weed, albeit an amaranthine weed
> Suffering no flowers except its own
>   to mount?"

How he had clung to the pleasures of fancy, on whose magic pinions he had soared

> "From star to star,
> From world to luminous world, as far
> As the universe spreads her flaming wall!"[5]

Can it be that he must give up all those lofty thoughts and imaginations which he considered a part of him-

[4] Francis Thompson, Shelley.
[5] Thomas Moore, Paradise and the Peri.

self? Will the Tremendous Lover root up all other loves in his heart's garden and usurp their place? 'Tis the old lament,

"Lest having Him I shall have naught beside."

Self-love and love of creatures is dying hard but—dying.

"Ah! must Thou char the wood ere Thou canst
limn with it?"

This question has been ringing through the ages since the fall of Adam, and, though answered every day, will be reiterated till the end of time; so slow is man to understand what things are for his good.

As Mansoul sees the futility of resistance, he no longer tries to "kick against the goad,"[6] but is willing to be an instrument in God's hands in order to carry out His wonderful designs. However, he is unwilling to undergo suffering in order to become such an instrument. Nor yet does he realize that a soul cannot be of service to God till it has passed through the fires of tribulation, yes, been tried as gold in the furnace. As only molten gold that has been purified of all dross can be moulded by the artificer into pleasing and beautiful forms, so only the soul that has been purified in the crucible, and thus rendered pliable to the fingers of the infinite Designer, can be of use to Him, to its neighbor and to itself. "Who suffers, conquers."[7] Suffering is the road to Heaven. If there were another or a better way Christ would have shown it in His life

[6] Acts. ix. 5.
[7] Francis Thompson, Moestitiae Encomium.

and in His words. From Bethlehem to Calvary was one long martyrdom. He tells us, "Blessed are those that mourn," "Blessed are they that suffer,"[8] "Deny thyself, take up thy cross and follow Me."[9]

Nothing great, even in the natural order, has been accomplished in the world except through suffering.

"Not a truth has to art or to science been given,
But brows have ached for it and souls toiled and
striven."[10]

How much more true is this of the supernatural order. No noble character is ever developed, no heights of sanctity reached, without sorrow and pain. "No man ever attained supreme knowledge unless his heart had been torn up by the roots."[11] If suffering were eliminated from our lives, joy would be unknown. "Pain may be made the instrument of joy."[12] But for suffering the beautiful virtues that make life endurable would never be called into action: patience, resignation, sympathy, kindness, charity.

Only those who have suffered, feel for the sufferings of others. Dido is made to say in Aeneid, *"Non ignara mali, miseris succurrere disco."*[13]

Trials and hardships are the tools which the Divine Artist uses in chiseling our characters and molding our souls more and more in conformity to His image and likeness.

[8] Matt. v. 5 and 10.
[9] Matt. xvi. 24.
[10] Owen Meredith, Lucile, Canto VI.
[11] Francis Thompson, Moestitiae Encomium.
[12] Francis Thompson, St. Francis.
[13] Virgil, The Aeneid, Book I, 1. 630.

Sufferings sent by God are the greatest proofs of His love, and sufferings offered up to Him, the greatest gift of His lovers.

In the lustihood of youth, Mansoul has wasted all the affections of his heart, all the powers of his mind, on unworthy objects, the perishable things of earth, "dust." His heart was as a limpid fountain in the midst of a seemingly beautiful garden, bright with verdure and exquisite flowers. How he delighted in its loveliness!

But now? His heart is emptied of its ardent affections, glowing hopes and high aspirations, which like sunlit waters refreshed with their sparkling spray everything around them; and is filled with gnawing remorse; yes, sad thoughts and bitter memories make of it,

> "a broken fount,
> Wherein tear-drippings stagnate spilt down ever
>   From the dank thoughts that shiver
>   Upon the sighful branches of my mind.
>   Such is; what is to be?
>   The pulp so bitter, how shall taste the rind?"

If the present is such an abyss of gloom and despair, what will the future be? No more "vistaed hopes" of interminable beauty and promise stretch out before him. An impenetrable forest of dark fears and anxieties block his view. Yet from present experiences, he can form some idea of what the misty future has in store for him in this world. Nothing but the canker worm of remorse. But Eternity? For the first time, he senses the awful import of the word. Never before had he al-

lowed his mind to dwell on it. He had reveled in the
rosy dreams of the joys of life, but now

> "Ever and anon a trumpet sounds
> From the dim battlements of Eternity!"

and while the awe-inspiring sound is ringing in his
ears, he catches a faint glimpse of that "mysterious
bourne whence no traveler returns,"[14] but between him
and Eternity he beholds the terrible form of Death the
summoner,

> "With glooming robes purpureal, cypress-
> crowned."

Death is repulsive to Mansoul, as he is to all those
who shun the thought of his existence, who do not
grow familiar with him and see in him a kind and
loving friend who is to free them from bondage and
bring them to their own country. Mansoul rebels at
the necessity of death and another bitter wail goes up
from the depths of that stricken heart,

> "Whether man's heart or life it be which yields
> Thee harvest, must Thy harvest-fields
> Be dunged with rotten death?"[15]

His heart has already yielded its harvest by the loss
of all his hopes and earthly joys, but he knows that
his life cannot yield its harvest until the fields "be
dunged with rotten death." Know you not, O purblind

---

[14] Shakespeare: Hamlet.
[15] "Did Christ manure thy heart to breed Him briers?
Or did it need this unaccustomed soyle
With hellish dung to fertile heaven's desires?"
Southwell.

soul, that death is the only portal of life, and that unless one first dies to himself he cannot live to God? Have you not noticed in your study of nature that life springs from death? "Unless the grain of wheat falling to the ground die, it itself remaineth alone. But if it die, it bringeth forth much fruit. He that loveth his life shall lose it; and he that hateth his life in this world, keepeth it unto life eternal."[16]

[16] John. xii. 24-25.

V

LOVE CONQUERS

NEVER in his mad flight had Mansoul stopped to consider the great truths of religion but now that he does think of them, they sink deep into his mind, crowding out less worthy thoughts and destroying within him the last vestige of self-love. Humbled and truly repentant, he yields himself completely to his faithful Lover,

"That Voice is round me like a bursting sea."

The gentle voice of the Master is no louder than before, but the heart of His wayward child is at last attuned to it, just as the waves of ether have always carried vibrations, but sounds were not reproduced till instruments attuned to them were made.

Now the soul listens eagerly to the Voice which says:

"And is thy earth so marred
Shattered in shard on shard?"

Mansoul sees his idols scattered like broken pottery around him, those idols he had worshipped so long; on which he had lavished his most ardent affections; and for which he had sacrificed his precious time, the golden coin given him by God to purchase eternal life. And what are they? Dust, nothing but dust and ashes.

What a humiliation for him to find himself so easily duped, to find that he had been chasing phantoms instead of realities! Humiliations, however, are the stepping-stones to humility, and humility is the foundation of perfection.

"Lo, all things fly thee for thou fliest Me."

As he who seeks first the Kingdom of God and His justice, has all things else added, so he that seeks the kingdom of the world and its injustice, has all things taken from him. Poor Mansoul has learned by sad experience the utter inability of creatures to satisfy his longings, but he has not yet fully recognized his own nothingness. In the crucible of suffering, however, he has been prepared for the knife which in the hands of the skilful Surgeon is to cut away the film from his eyes and let him see himself as he is. Base flatterers have deluded him into the belief that he is worthy of love and admiration, worthy of having his name written in the hearts of men and his deeds recorded in their memory. Now from the loving lips that never deceive, he hears

> "Strange, piteous, futile thing,
>   Wherefore should any set thee love apart,
>   Seeing none but I make much of naught,"
>   And human love needs human meriting:
>   How hast thou merited—
>   Of all man's clotted clay the dingiest clot?
>   Alack, thou knowest not
>   How little worthy of any love thou art!
>   Whom wilt thou find to love ignoble thee
>   Save Me, save only Me?"

Thus the Divine Friend holds the mirror up to the soul, that for the first time sees himself as he really is, an object of pity, not of love. He wonders that he could ever have looked for the esteem of men when he is nothing else but nothing. What has he done to merit love? He thought only of self and self-gratification. Men are not inclined to give their affection gratis. It must be bought and often at a great price.

At last the proud spirit lies prostrate, humbled to the dust, crushed by the weight of its own nothingness, and now he can truly say,

"Naked I wait Thy love's uplifted stroke."

Stripped of all things, even of self, he is ready for whatever God may see fit to send him, knowing himself to be worthy only of chastisement. Pride has given place to humility; rebellion, to submission; fear, to perfect trust and confidence; love of creatures, to love of the Creator. God's love is all-sufficient now and with St. Ignatius, he cries out "Grant me only Thy love and Thy grace and I am rich enough; I ask nothing more."[1]

The Divine Lover will not be outdone in generosity and in sweet consoling words, promises to the poor prodigal all that He had taken from him,

"All which thy child's mistake
Fancies as lost, I have stored for thee at home."

How sweet, how tender the assurance! Friendship had seemed to Mansoul the dearest thing on earth; its purest joys will be his without measure in Heaven. He will have as his friends all the Blessed and above all,

[1] St. Ignatius, Suscipe.

the Changeless Friend who has been true to him through all the vicissitudes of life, and who will love him through all Eternity.

The glories of nature which so captivated him, will be found there in all their perfection for "Absolute nature lives not in our life nor yet is lifeless but lives in the life of God. She is God's daughter. Is this daughter of God mortal? Can her foot not pass the grave? Is Nature, as men tell us, but a veil concealing the eternal,

> ' . . . a fold
> Of Heaven and earth across His Face?'

which man must rend to behold that Face? Do our eyes indeed close forever on the beauty of earth when they open to the beauty of Heaven? I think not so: I believe that in Heaven is earth. Plato's doctrine of Ideals as I conceive, laid its hand upon the very breast of truth yet missed her breathing. Within the Spirit who is Heaven lies Earth; for within Him are the great conceptions of Creation."[2]

He loves children. He will find in the Blessed all the attractive, appealing qualities of children: simplicity, guilelessness, joyousness of spirit.

Poetry and Beauty in their perfection are awaiting him at Home. Beauty is there for "Beauty is truth, truth, beauty; and the fruits of beauty, poetry and music, for poetry is in itself a thing of God."[3] Yes, the "linked fantasies" that at times made the earth a paradise for him, will never more be broken by the weight of sorrow and sin, but will be a perennial source of joy and gladness.

[2] Francis Thompson. Nature's Immortality.
[3] Bailey.

All these blessings has his heavenly Father stored for him at home, and more, far more. He will not only restore the lost, but will bestow upon the penitent treasures that in his highest flights of fancy he never dreamed of. Not only will he enjoy eternally the gifts of God but will possess God Himself in an ineffable manner in the Beatific Vision. "Eye hath not seen, ear hath not heard, neither hath it entered into the heart of man to conceive what things God hath prepared for them that love Him."[4]

The soul, a short while ago so crushed and bruised, is revivified by the sweet balm of consolation, inebriated with a happiness it has never known before, "a peace which surpasseth all understanding." The "broken fount" is renewed, ready to receive the limpid waters of God's love which will cause the "sighful branches" of his mind to bud forth beautiful thoughts which lift one to the level of the angels. Now he knows that all his disappointments, all his sorrows, are but the

"Shade of His hand outstretched caressingly."

How eagerly he listens for that Voice, which once a torment to him, is now like the music of many waters,

"I am He whom thou seekest!
Thou dravest love from thee, who dravest Me."

Mansoul had spent the best years of his life in searching for the love and happiness that were within his grasp, like the man who traveled the world over looking for a rare and beautiful flower, and at last re-

[4] I Cor. ii. 9.

turned wearied and disheartened with his futile efforts, to his home to find the object of his quest growing at his cottage-door—the flower of contentment. So Man-soul finds at his door the happiness he had sought else-where in vain, for God is love and love is happiness.

How welcome the loving invitation,

> "Rise, clasp My hand and come."

It is only an invitation, there is no coercion, God does not lift him up and lead him away. He leaves him free as He has always done. But can he refuse? "Rise from the depths of misery into which you have been plunged; from the slough of despondency and despair, to the sun-kissed heights with their life-giving air, where you walked with Me in your innocent childhood. Clasp My hand that you may walk securely, that you may not fall into the snares and pitfalls on the way, or be drawn aside by the siren voices that would lead you to destruc-tion. Come. Whither? Wherever My grace leads you. Follow My will and you shall find rest to your soul. Together we shall climb, steep and rocky though the road may be, and ere long reach the sapphire gates which will open to admit you to your heavenly home."

Eagerly the purified soul, burning with love and gratitude, grasps the proffered hand, and free from the burdens that weighed him down and from the shackles that bound him to earth, walks joyously by the side of his loving Father, minding not the thorns and briers that beset his path, heeding not the fierce storm-clouds that gather, fearing not the wild beasts that glare at him. Trusting in the fatherly care of his Guide, he exclaims, "Thy will, O Lord, is my pleasure. Lead on whithersoever Thou wilt, I follow." "O Beauty ever ancient and ever new, too late have I known Thee, too late have I loved Thee."[5] "The chase of 'The Hound of Heaven' ends in a divine embrace."[6]

[5] Saint Augustine.
[6] Everard Meynell, Life of Francis Thompson.

VI

IS THE POEM A PERSONAL REVELATION?

ON reading "The Hound of Heaven," one is apt to speculate as to whether or no the soul portrayed in it is that of the poet. Could anyone describe so vividly the thoughts, feelings, aspirations, sufferings of another? Some answer emphatically, "No. It must be autobiographical." They even go so far as to wrench the poet's meaning so as to adapt the story to a Francis Thompson who is a figment of their own brain, a Francis Thompson who is as far removed from our conception of the gentle poet as pole from pole. They make him a creature of circumstances, a weakling carried along by every wind of passion, a fugitive from God and His love, a lover of himself, of pleasure, of fame.

Those who know and love him protest strongly against the injustice done him and his exquisite lyric. The poem, however, takes its coloring from the tastes, inclinations, character of the poet, and what glorious coloring it is, "A light that never was on sea or land."[1] "In all his poetry there is personal revelation, his own experience being the invisible wind that moves the cloudy pageant of his verse."[2]

It is very interesting, however, to note the resem-

[1] Wordsworth, On a Picture of Peele Castle in a Storm.
[2] Everard Meynell, The Life of Francis Thompson.

blances and contrasts between Francis and the "Soul."
They delighted in the same things: friendship, beauty,
poetry, children and nature; but with a difference. Mansoul loved all these things for their own sake, made
them ends not means to an end, the material meant
more to him than the spiritual. To Francis, material
things were meaningless until he saw in them the work
of the Divine Author. Mansoul longed for human affection, pleaded at "many a hearted casement" for admittance. Francis never sought the friendship of his
fellow-beings; they sought him and his love, and being
once admitted into the charmed circle, were true, de
voted, loyal to the end.

Wilfred and Alice Meynell, who took the poor out-
cast into their hearts and home and raised him to a
position of dignity and honor, resented the title of
benefactors, insisting that all obligation was on their
side. They considered themselves favored, honored by
his friendship. What happiness communion with such
rare and beautiful souls must have afforded him! Mr.
Charles L. O'Donnell says of them, "Mr. Meynell's
name, owing to the fact that it is worn also by Alice
Thompson Meynell, stands for all that is finest and
purest, most exalted and conservative in literature, in
art and in life. It stands also for what is best in lay
virtue, for both Mr. and Mrs. Meynell are practical
Catholics, with religious natures one with that spirit
of refined sanctity possessed by Coventry Patmore. In
fact, Mr. Wilfred Meynell has always seemed a sort
of lay Cardinal Newman, and Mrs. Meynell an English Eugénie de Guérin."[3]

[3] O'Donnell, Francis Thompson: A Critical Essay.

Through the influence of these devoted friends, Francis was brought in touch with Coventry Patmore with whom he formed a most delightful and helpful friendship, as also with Catherine Tynan, Katherine Douglas King, George Meredith, Alfred Hayes, Lewis Hind and others of the aristocracy of genius. Among the most valued of these were "the bearded counsellors of God,"[4] Fathers Anselm and Alphonso, worthy followers of the humble St. Francis, who were not without influence on the poet's later work.

Much as he enjoyed the inspiring and uplifting intercourse with all these chosen souls; much as he appreciated the depth and warmth of their affection, he never allowed human attachments to draw him away from God. He himself tells us, "All human love was to me a symbol of divine love."[5] "In human passion as in sun-worship he relates everything to the Deity. It is within forbidden degree if it cannot be referred to Divine Love."[6] That God always came first with him is shown by the following lines selected from different poems:

"Because I am so true
    My Fair, to Heaven, I am so true to you."[7]

"Beyond your trueness, Lady, Truth stands
        true."[8]

"O be true
    To your soul, dearest, as my life to you."[9]

[4] Francis Thompson.
[5] Meynell, Life of Francis Thompson.
[6] Ibid.   [7] Francis Thompson, A Holocaust.
[8] Francis Thompson, Ultimum.
[9] Francis Thompson, Manus Animam Pinxit.

He evinced his gratitude in his verse which was the medium for the expression of his emotions. Coventry Patmore says: "The heroic faith in and devotion to the interests of his genius which through long years has been shown by at least two friends, one of them a lady not inferior in genius to his own, his recognition of her helpfulness by a series of poems which St. John of the Cross might have addressed to St. Teresa . . . are all circumstances which will probably do more for his immediate acceptance by the literary public than qualities which ought to place him in the permanent ranks of fame with Cowley and Crashaw."[10]

In "To W. M.," speaking of himself as a grafted branch, Francis says:

"That one branch
Shall cling to thee, my Father, Brother, Friend,
Shall cling to thee until the end of end."

Patmore's friendship for Francis Thompson was sincere and deep, as the following passage from a letter written to Francis at Pantasaph will show: "If at any time you find yourself seriously ill and do not find the attendance, food, etc., sufficiently good, tell me and I will go to Pantasaph to take care of you for any time you might find me useful. It would be a great pleasure and honor to serve you in any way." The following remark in Thompson's answer, "I can truly say that I never yet fell from any friend that did not first fall from me," would seem to imply that some friend or friends had abandoned him, but we know of none except the little girl of the street who had be-

[10] *Fortnightly Review*, July, 1894.

friended him, and vanished from his life when he no longer needed assistance. The unfortunate estrangement from his own family on account of a misunderstanding could hardly have been meant. *Fortunate* we should call it, yes, a wise dispensation of Providence, as the suffering it brought upon Francis, gave to the world its great poet.

The poet, like Mansoul, loved beauty. He found it everywhere, in everything, from the starry firmament to "the meanest flower that blows."[11] Beauty never refused him admittance; he did not smite in vain "the gold gateways of the stars" because, unlike Mansoul, "He saw through the lamp Beauty, the light, God."[12] The loveliness of creatures was to him but a faint fleeting reflection of the beauty of the Creator. Instead of attaching his heart to the earth, it raised his thoughts to Heaven, its home. There he hoped to find the beauty of this world immortalized.

"Beauty, such is my faith, is beauty for Eternity."[13]

The passage in "The Hound of Heaven":

"Across the margent of the world I fled,
    And troubled the gold gateways of the stars,
    Smiting for shelter on their clangèd bars"[14]

is by some, after a cursory reading, interpreted as the soul's insatiable desire for worldly glory; they insist that like Aeneas, Mansoul wished his fame to reach the stars. Were such an interpretation possible, the

[11] Wordsworth, Intimations of Immortality.
[12] Francis Thompson, Shelley.
[13] Francis Thompson, Nature's Immortality.   [14] Lines 25-27.

passage could not apply to Thompson. He says of himself in "The Dead Cardinal of Westminster,"

> "He lives detachèd days,
>   He serveth not for praise,
>   For gold
>   He is not sold.
> Deaf is he to world's tongue,
>   He scorneth for his song
>   The loud
>   Shouts of the crowd.
> He asketh not world's eyes,
>   Not to world's ears he cries,
>   Saith—'These
>   Shut if you please.' "

He reveled, as did Mansoul, in the elysian fields of Poesy "The long savannahs of the blue"; "Clung to the whistling mane of every wind" and like Shelley, "grew gold-dusty from rolling among the stars."[15]

Well might he rejoice in the great gift God had bestowed upon him, "A rarer, more intense, more strictly predestinate genius has never been known to man."[16] What Francis Thompson said of Shelley, may be applied to himself, "His choruses sweep down the wind tirelessly, flight after flight, till the breathless soul almost cries for respite from the unrolling splendors."[17] Mr. George Shuster speaks of his poetry as having a peculiarly Gothic nature as evidenced by "the verve with which it sweeps to airy pinnacles in the dizzy blue of the skies.[18]

[15] Francis Thompson, Shelley.   [16] Garvin, Bookman.
[17] Francis Thompson, Shelley.
[18] Shuster, The Catholic Spirit in Modern Literature.

Coventry Patmore calls him "A Titan among recent poets," and Arnold Bennett says, "My belief is that Francis Thompson has a richer natural genius, a finer poetical equipment than any poet since Shakespeare."[19]

His wonderful gift was a great consolation to him, as it was a vent, an escape valve for his emotions. "Deep grief or pain has in my case found immediate outlet in poetry."[20] That he felt within himself the sweet assurance that his verse was immortal, is evident from the following passages:

> "I hang mid men my needless head,
>   And my fruit is dreams as theirs is bread.
>   The goodly men and the sun-hazed sleeper
>   Time shall reap, but after the reaper,
>   The world shall glean of me, me the sleeper."[21]

> "I sprinkled a few drops of verse
>   And said to Ruin, 'Quit thy hearse';
>   To my loved 'Pale not, come with me,
>   I will escort thee down the years
>   With me thou walkest immortally.' "[22]

He shared with Mansoul the fear of losing

> "The linked fantasies in whose blossomy twist
>   I swung the earth a trinket at my wrist."[23]

To his friend, Wilfred Meynell, he writes. "With this volume I am probably closing my brief poetic career." In "Proemion," "My Songs' sands like the

[19] *Woman.* July, 1893.
[20] Francis Thompson. In Meynell's Life of Thompson.
[21] Ibid.   [22] Ibid. Proemion.
[23] Ibid. The Hound of Heaven.

Year's are few, but take this last weak gift from me."
Comparing his case to the earth's life in winter, "tear-
less beneath the frost-scorched sod," he says

> "My lips have drought and cracked
>   By laving music long unvisited."[24]

"In exquisite lines he begs his muse to stay their flight,
and his exquisite lines belie the convention that they
have flown, that the shrines of his heart are empty . . .
He lost not the poetry but the function of the poet.[25]
His regret at the loss of his poetic powers seemed to
arise from the fact that he has no longer a fit medium
for the expression of his gratitude to his friends,

> "Ah! gone are the days when for undying
>   kindness
> I still could render you undying song."[26]

Though he felt keenly the supposed dying out of the
divine fire, there was no murmuring against the de-
crees of an all-wise Providence. He knew that "Poetry
is a thing of God." If God wished to take what belonged
to Him, why should he complain? He considered poetry
as having a divine mission and while his wonderful
powers remained in their fulness, he used them for
their God-given purpose. "That should be precisely the
function of poetry, to see and restore the divine idea
of things." "To be the poet of the return to nature is
somewhat but I would be the poet of the return to
God."[27]

---

[24] Francis Thompson, From the Night of Forebeing.
[25] Everard Meynell, Life of Francis Thompson.
[26] Francis Thompson, Lines to W. M. A Double Need.
[27] Francis Thompson, Pico della Mirandola.

So imbued are his poems with the spiritual that were it eliminated, there would be nothing but the skeleton left. "Through all his works the spiritual element is the one commanding indubitable thing."[28]

Though many passages might be cited to confirm the correctness of the interpretation of the lines:

"To all swift things for swiftness did I sue;
Clung to the whistling mane of every wind"

as referring to the wonderful flights of fancy; as for instance, the one already quoted from Shelley, and this from the same essay: "His thoughts became as mounted infantry passing with baffling swiftness from horse to foot, from foot to horse," there are some who insist that these lines prove that the soul was making a mad rush after this world's pleasures. Charles L. O'Donnell makes this interpretation, and considering the poem autobiographical, applies them to Francis Thompson, "Down those few terrible years he let himself go with the winds of fancy and threw himself on the swelling waves of every passion, desiring only to live to the full."[29] Even were the interpretation correct, the application is not. Alice Meynell declares that Francis Thompson "was one of the most innocent of men."[30] George Shuster says of him: "Of all the poets of later years he is the one who guarded best the citadel of his soul." After all, he had nothing to regret in the manner of his life—Francis was the disciple of sanctity. . . . In the ordinary sense he had not sinned against the light, but kept his soul bright as it had been in child-

[28] Katherine Bregy: The Poets' Chantry.
[29] Charles L. O'Donnell, Francis Thompson, A Critical Essay.
[30] Dublin Review. Jan. 1908.

hood. . . . "Who can analyze a soul so patient, so reverent, so governed by the best instincts of childhood?"[31] In "The Dead Cardinal of Westminster" Francis says of himself:

> "He measureth world's pleasures
> World's ease as saints might measure."

Then, too, "No truly morbid heart has ever been known to delight in children."[32] His reverent love for children is manifested in the line:

> "The heart of childhood so divine for me."[33]

Some of his most beautiful poems were inspired by "the sweet feat ways" of childhood. In "To Stars" he says:

> "Two child eyes have dulled a firmament for me."

In "To Olivia,"

> "I fear to love thee, Sweet, because
> Love's the ambassador of loss."

and in "Daisy,"

> "O there were flowers in springtime
> On the turf and on the spray,
> But the sweetest flower on Sussex Hills
> Was the Daisy flower that day.
>
> *   *   *   *   *   *
>
> She went her unremembering ways
> She went and left to me
> The pang of all the partings gone
> And partings yet to be."

[31] George Shuster, The Catholic Spirit in Modern Literature.
[32] Katherine Bregy, The Poets' Chantry.
[33] Sister Songs, Part One.

"Sister Songs," the most exquisite lyric in the language next to Shakespeare's Sonnets, was inspired by the children he loved so well, Monica and Madeline (Sylvia) Meynell. "It is the poet's love of love in the abstract, revealed to him symbolically in the tender youth of two little girls."[34]

In his exquisite essay on Shelley, Francis says: "Know you not what it is to be a child? It is to have a spirit yet streaming from the waters of Baptism; it is to believe in love, to believe in loveliness, to believe in belief; it is

> 'To see a world in a grain of sand
> And a heaven in a wild flower,
> Hold infinity in the palm of the hand,
> And Eternity in an hour.' "

Why multiply instances to prove his love for God's little ones, we know it from one line,

> "Look for me in the nurseries of Heaven."[35]

He grieves, as Mansoul did, when the angel plucked the children from him by the hair. He frequently expressed the regret that childhood is so fleeting, as in "Absence":

> "Canst thou be what thou hast been?
> No, no more what thou hast!
> Lo, all last things that I have known
> And all that shall be last
> Went past
> With the thing thou wast."

[34] Le Galliene, "The Star."　　[35] To My Godchild.

In "Sister Songs" he says to Sylvia:

> "Over thy form, dear child, alas my art
>   Cannot prevail; but immortalizing touch
> I lay upon thy heart."

We have already quoted one instance from "To Monica after Nine Years" ending with

> "But where are you, child, *you*?"

In the same poem he says:

> "There was one
>   Shall no more beneath the sun
>   Darkle, fondle, featly play.
> If to think on her be gloom,
> Rejoice she has so rich a tomb.
> But there's he—
> Ask not who it may be
> That until Time's boughs are bare
> Shall be unconsoled for her."

Miss King, who did much charitable work among poor sick children, wrote Francis after a visit he had paid to the Orphan Asylum: "I think of you now with that infant's serious confiding face upturned to you. To some people a child is a pretty ornamental addition. Your personality now seems incomplete without the child as the natural and exquisite finish to the whole man."

The words of Hawthorne may aptly be applied to him: "Lingering always so near his childhood, he had sympathies with children and kept his heart the fresher thereby like a reservoir into which rivulets are flowing not far from the fountain-head."

Nature was a perennial delight to him. His "Songs of Nature" are

"Sweet with wild wings that pass that pass away";[36]

Yet he loved it not for its own sake. He would praise the

"Giver of spring and song and every young new
        thing."[37]

His biographer, Everard Meynell, says, "Nature he ignored till she spoke the language of religion"; also: "Let him see but one sunset and the daily mystery of that going down would companion him for a lifetime; let him see but one daisy and all his paths would be strewn with white and gold."[38]

He loved the flowers, the groves, the hills, the streams, but he loved the "crystal Heaven's magic sphere"[39] best of all. He walked with his head among the stars when his feet were in the gutter, so he was kept unspotted from the world. What Byron said of the ocean, can more truthfully be said of the sky:

"Boundless, endless and sublime,
    The image of Eternity,—the throne
    Of the Invisible."[40]

Always fair and unsullied it remains, ever changing yet ever the same. The sun was to Francis an image of the Deity.

[36] Francis Thompson, Ode to the Setting Sun—Prelude.
[37] Francis Thompson, The Night of Forebeing.
[38] Everard Meynell, Life of Francis Thompson.
[39] Francis Thompson, A Corymbus for Autumn.
[40] Byron, Apostrophe to Ocean.

"Thou dost image, thou dost follow
That King-Maker of Creation
Who ere Hellas hailed Apollo,
Gave thee, angel-god, thy station.
Thou art of Him a type memorial
Like Him thou hangest in dreadful pomp of blood
Upon thy Western Rood."[41]

His own words prove that He "Looks through Nature up to Nature's God."[42] "The intellect of man seems unable to seize the divine beauty of nature until moving beyond that outward beauty it gazes on the spirit of nature,"[43]

"Oh, gaze ye on the firmament, a hundred clouds in
                    motion
Up-piled in the immense sublime beneath the wind's
                    commotion,
O contemplate the heavens when the vein-drawn day
                    dies pale
In every season, every place gaze through their every
                    veil."[44]

Beneath their solemn beauty is a mystery infinite.
Francis, like the soul he depicted, suffered.

"He learned in suffering what he taught in song."[45]

As Mansoul sent forth the wail:
"Ah, must Thou char the wood ere Thou canst limn
        with it?"

[41] Francis Thompson, The Setting Sun.
[42] Pope, Essay on Man.
[43] Francis Thompson, Paganism, Old and New.
[44] Francis Thompson, A Sunset.
[45] Shelley, Julian and Maddalo.

so Francis "Is there no drinking of pearls except they be dissolved in biting tears?"[46] Yet he was unembittered, did not question God's right to send him suffering. He knew well, too, that a world without suffering is a world without joy. In his "Commentaries on St. Francis," he says: "Pain which came to man as a penalty, remains with him as a consecration. . . . Pain may be made the instrument of joy. . . . There is no special love without special pain."

Francis suffered from want, neglect, cold and hunger, many pains of body and mind; but his greatest suffering probably was caused by his super-sensitive nature, his reticence, which prevented his seeking solace from others.

> "The once accursed star that did me teach
> To make of silence my familiar."[47]

He felt the powerlessness of language to express deep feeling. "When we can communicate ourselves by words, it may often become a sensible effort to a sensitive person through the more dead weight of language, the gross actualities of speech."[48]

We surely have abundant proof that Francis never fled God and His love, that is, consciously, deliberately, continually. His whole life belies such an accusation: his innocent childhood and youth; his aspirations to the priesthood; the blamelessness of his conduct during the years of want and misery in the London streets; the

[46] Francis Thompson, Shelley.
[47] Francis Thompson: Quoted in Meynell's *Life of Francis Thompson.*
[48] Francis Thompson, in a letter to Mrs. Meynell.

love and admiration of the friends who rescued him
and found his character pure gold, made all the brighter
by the fires of tribulation through which he had passed;
above all, his intense love of God, his reverence for
all things holy as manifested in his works. "The argu-
ment of the poet's sanctity is in his poems."[49] "He believed supremely in God and he believed in stepping-
stones up which the soul might hope to climb, down
which God Himself must peradventure descend."[50]
Patmore declares, "He is of all men I know most
naturally a Catholic." Francis himself did not doubt
his position as a churchman. "His work is most mem-
orable for its essential Catholicity, its spiritual pro-
fundity and elevation."[51] "The personal embrace
between Creator and creature is so solely the secret and
note of Catholicity that its language to the outer sects
is simply unintelligible."[52]

He was instinctively religious. Religion was a part
of his very being. He would not have been Francis
Thompson without it. Every note-book from his boyhood had in it some device that showed the spiritual
bent of his mind. He said his prayers so devoutly, so
earnestly, indeed so solemnly, that his landlady de-
clared that one would think he was preaching; and
sometimes said such long grace that the dishes would
get cold. The Bible was to him a never-failing fountain
of joy. "Its influence was mystical; it revealed to me

---

[49] Everard Meynell, Life of Francis Thompson. "In propor-
tion to the height of their sanctity the saints are inevitable
poets. Sanctity is essential song." Francis Thompson on reading St. Bernard's translations.

[50] Katherine Bregy, The Poets' Chantry.   [51] Ibid.

[52] Francis Thompson.

a whole scheme of existence and lit up life like a lantern."[53]

Mr. George Shuster says of him: "Most important among Thompson's qualities was the seer's hearkening to the heart-beats of Truth, the mystic reading of a manifold script written to spell out the Word. . . . He served two queens, Beauty and Truth with his life."[54]

Wilfrid Meynell in a protest against a criticism of Francis Thompson in "The Times," just after the poet's death, writes: "No pen, least of all mine—can do justice to him; to his rectitude, to his gentleness, to his genius; . . . If he had great misfortunes, he bore them greatly; they were great because everything about him was great."[55]

[53] Francis Thompson: Letter quoted in Meynell's *Life of Francis Thompson.*
[54] The Catholic Spirit in Modern Literature.
[55] *The Nation*, November, 1907.

CONCLUSION

WE enter upon the study of "The Hound of Heaven" with diffidence, akin to fear; we pursue it with love and eagerness; we leave it with regret, with that indescribable feeling one has at the close of a retreat. We are grateful to the sweet singer for the beauty of his song, but more grateful for its elevating influence, for the spiritual good one derives from it.

We have learned that the soul whose experience it relates, is not an ordinary soul; it has noble instincts, high ideals; it loves the best that the world can give, the richest earthly gifts of God to man: friendship, beauty, poetry, childhood and nature. Dazzled by the brightness of the gifts, it beholds not the Giver. But when the veil is snatched from its eyes and it sees the Author of all good, the ardent soul forgets everything else and throws itself into its Father's arms.

High-minded though this soul may be, it is not the soul of Francis Thompson, for he walked with God, saw His beauty in every leaf and blossom—

> "From sky to sod
> The world's unfolded blossom smells of God"[1]

heard His gentle voice in every light breeze and felt His wrath in the thunder's peal; he beheld His grandeur and majesty and beneficence in His ambassador the sun, and His glory in the starry Heavens.

[1] Francis Thompson, The Night of Forebeing.

His songs are so redolent of divine things, so full of God and His attributes, that one feels like reversing his expression, and saying:

Song is essential sanctity.

It is said that Shakespeare dealt with the things of time and Dante with those of Eternity; so it may be said that Thompson deals with the relation between the two. "The Hound of Heaven" is the best example of this. Francis's glory will no doubt be increased for all eternity for having written this wonderful poem whose enlightening, inspiring lines should aid in leading many souls to God.

That Francis Thompson valued holiness of life without genius, far more than genius without holiness, is evident, especially so in "A Judgment in Heaven." A poet, "roseate-crowned and splendent-vested" and a poor rhymer in poetical tatters, appear together before the Judgment-seat of God. The poet beholds the saint in the rhymer, and throwing off his own garb of genius seems no richer than the other. The All-seeing Eye penetrates the disguise of both,

"Fetch forth the Paradisal garb! spake the
    Father sweet and low,
Drew them both by the frightened hand where
Mary's throne made irised bow—
Take, Princess Mary, of thy good grace, two
Spirits greater than they know."

We trust that our dear poet has received such a welcome in Heaven; that he now sees face to face that God whom he knew and loved through the mirror of His works; yes, that this man who in the midst of degradation, of sin, kept his soul pure and bright as a diamond buried in the slime of the earth; that this "poet of the return to God," the most guileless perhaps of all uncanonized poets, is now enjoying the Beatific Vision.

Bibliography

Holy Scripture. Job—Jeremias—The Gospels—Psalms

Everard Meynell. The Life of Francis Thompson

Katherine Bregy. The Poets' Chantry

Louis Garvin. The Bookman

George Shuster. The Catholic Spirit in Modern Literature

Rev. J. P. X. O'Connor S.J. The Hound of Heaven—A Study

Rev. Francis Le Buffe S.J. The Hound of Heaven—An Interpretation

Francis Thompson. Poems Vol. I and II. Prose Vol. III. Charles Scribner's Sons.

PRINTED BY BENZIGER BROTHERS, NEW YORK

THE HOUND OF HEAVEN

I FLED Him, down the nights and down the days;
  I fled Him, down the arches of the years;
I fled Him, down the labyrinthine ways
  Of my own mind; and in the midst of tears
I hid from Him, and under running laughter.   5
      Up vistaed hopes, I sped;
      And shot, precipitated,
A-down Titanic glooms of chasmèd fears,
  From those strong Feet that followed, followed after.
      But with unhurrying chase,   10
      And unperturbèd pace,
    Deliberate speed, majestic instancy,
      They beat—and a Voice beat
      More instant than the Feet—
  "All things betray thee, who betrayest Me."   15

      I pleaded, outlaw-wise,
By many a hearted casement, curtained red,
  Trellised with intertwining charities;
(For, though I knew His love Who followed,
    Yet was I sore adread   20
Lest, having Him, I must have naught beside);
But, if one little casement parted wide,
  The gust of His approach would clash it to.
  Fear wist not to evade as Love wist to pursue.
Across the margent of the world I fled,   25
  And troubled the gold gateways of the stars,

Smiting for shelter on their clangèd bars;
    Fretted to dulcet jars
And silvern chatter the pale ports o' the moon.
I said to dawn: Be sudden—to eve: Be soon;   30
  With thy young skyey blossoms heap me over
    From this tremendous Lover!
Float thy vague veil about me, lest He see!
  I tempted all His servitors, but to find
My own betrayal in their constancy,   35
In faith to Him their fickleness to me,
  Their traitorous trueness, and their loyal deceit.
To all swift things for swiftness did I sue;
  Clung to the whistling mane of every wind.
      But whether they swept, smoothly fleet,   40
    The long savannahs of the blue;
      Or whether, Thunder-driven,
    They clanged His chariot 'thwart a heaven
Plashy with flying lightnings round the spurn o' their
    feet:—
Fear wist not to evade as Love wist to pursue.   45
      Still with unhurrying chase,
      And unperturbèd pace,
    Deliberate speed, majestic instancy,
      Came on the following Feet,
      And a Voice above their beat—   50
  "Naught shelters thee, who wilt not shelter Me."

I sought no more that after which I strayed,
    In face of man or maid;
But still within the little children's eyes
  Seems something, something that replies,   55
They at least are for me, surely for me!

I turned me to them very wistfully;
But just as their young eyes grew sudden fair
    With dawning answers there,
Their angel plucked them from me by the hair.   60
"Come then, ye other children, Nature's—share
With me" (said I) "your delicate fellowship;
  Let me greet you lip to lip,
  Let me twine with you caresses,
      Wantoning   65
  With our Lady-Mother's vagrant tresses,
      Banqueting
  With her in her wind-walled palace,
    Underneath her azured daïs,
  Quaffing, as your taintless way is,   70
    From a chalice
Lucent-weeping out of the day-spring."
      So it was done:
I in their delicate fellowship was one—
Drew the bolt of Nature's secrecies.   75
  I knew all the swift importings
  On the wilful face of skies;
  I knew how the clouds arise
    Spumèd of the wild sea-snortings;
    All that's born or dies   80
Rose and drooped with—made them shapers
Of mine own moods, or wailful or divine—
  With them joyed and was bereaven.
  I was heavy with the even,
When she lit her glimmering tapers   85
  Round the day's dead sanctities.
  I laughed in the morning's eyes.

I triumphed and I saddened with all weather,
    Heaven and I wept together,
And its sweet tears were salt with mortal mine;   90
Against the red throb of its sunset-heart
      I laid my own to beat,
        And share commingling heat;
But not by that, by that, was eased my human smart.
In vain my tears were wet on Heaven's grey check. 95
For, ah! we know not what each other says,
    These things and I; in sound *I* speak—
Their sound is but their stir, they speak by silences.
Nature, poor stepdame, cannot slake my drouth;
    Let her, if she would owe me,   100
Drop yon blue bosom-veil of sky, and show me
    The breasts of her tenderness:
Never did any milk of hers once bless
      My thirsting mouth.
      Nigh and nigh draws the chase,   105
      With unperturbed pace,
    Deliberate speed, majestic instancy,
      And past those noisèd Feet
      A Voice comes yet more fleet—
    "Lo! naught contents thee, who content'st not Me."

Naked I wait Thy love's uplifted stroke!   111
My harness piece by piece Thou hast hewn from me,
    And smitten me to my knee;
    I am defenceless utterly.
    I slept, methinks and woke   115
And, slowly gazing, find me stripped in sleep.
In the rash lustihead of my young powers,
    I shook the pillaring hours

And pulled my life upon me; grimed with smears,
I stand amid the dust o' the mounded years—   120
My mangled youth lies dead beneath the heap.
My days have crackled and gone up in smoke,
Have puffed and burst as sun starts on a stream.
    Yea, faileth now even dream
The dreamer, and the lute the lutanist;   125
Even the linked fantasies, in whose blossomy twist
I swung the earth a trinket at my wrist,
Are yielding; cords of all too weak account
For earth with heavy griefs so overplussed.
    Ah! is Thy love indeed   130
A weed, albeit an amaranthine weed,
Suffering no flowers except its own to mount?
    Ah! must—
      Designer Infinite!—
Ah! must Thou char the wood ere Thou canst limn 135
    with it?
My freshness spent its wavering shower i' the dust;
And now my heart is as a broken fount,
Wherein tear-drippings stagnate, spilt down ever
    From the dank thoughts that shiver
Upon the sighful branches of my mind.   140
    Such is; what is to be?
The pulp so bitter, how shall taste the rind?
I dimly guess what Time in mists confounds;
Yet ever and anon a trumpet sounds
From the hid battlements of Eternity: 145
Those shaken mists a space unsettle, then
Round the half-glimpsed turrets slowly wash again;
    But not ere him who summoneth
    I first have seen, enwound

With glooming robes purpureal, cypress-crowned; 150
His name I know, and what his trumpet saith.
Whether man's heart or life it be which yields
    Thee harvest, must Thy harvest fields
    Be dunged with rotten death?
    Now of that long pursuit   155
    Comes on at hand the bruit;
That Voice is round me like a bursting sea;
    "And is thy earth so marred,
    Shattered in shard on shard?
Lo, all things fly thee, for thou fliest Me!   160
    Strange, piteous, futile thing!
Wherefore should any set thee love apart?
Seeing none but I make much of naught" (He said),
"And human love needs human meriting:
    How hast thou merited—   165
Of all man's clotted clay, the dingiest clot?
    Alack, thou knowest not
How little worthy of any love thou art!
Whom wilt thou find to love ignoble thee,
    Save Me, save only Me?   170
All which I took from thee I did but take,
    Not for thy harms,
But just that thou might'st seek it in My arms.
    All which thy child's mistake
Fancies as lost, I have stored for thee at home: 175
    Rise, clasp My hand, and come."
    Halts by me that footfall:
    Is my gloom, after all,
    Shade of His hand, outstretched caressingly?
    "Ah! fondest, blindest, weakest,   180
    I am He Whom thou seekest!
Thou dravest love from thee, who dravest Me."